Laurel

So long as we enjoy the light of day
may we greet one another with love.

So long as we enjoy the light of day
may we pray for one another.

Zuni

ONE EARTH, ONE SPIRIT

A child's book of prayers from many faiths and cultures

Compiled by Tessa Strickland

Sierra Club Books for Children
San Francisco

FOREWORD

Every faith and culture has its own way of praying: some people dance; some kneel or sit; and others create sacred art or music. Many people regard certain occasions and particular times of day, such as the morning and evening, as the best times to pray. And often people come together, either as families or communities, to pray, as well as praying alone. Whenever we pray, we acknowledge that our lives are part of a mystery that is greater than we can understand. This mystery is not separate from us; it is all around and inside us.

In many cultures, there are prayers for every activity you can think of, because all of life is seen as sacred, and every living thing—whether an insect, a bird, a river, or a field of corn—is considered sacred, too. The prayers in this book show us that everything we do is connected with the world around us. Most of them are ancient, but all express feelings that we can recognize. Some of the prayers are requests; some are words of thanksgiving; some are blessings; and some are simply prayers of joy and celebration. But even though they come from many different times and places, all of them offer us ways to discover the spirit that breathes life into the changing beauty of the natural world. The photographs that illustrate the prayers also show us something of this beauty, helping us to see that whoever we are and whatever we believe, we all can use prayers to enrich our lives.

The soul that is not nourished by prayer
Is like a tree without soil.
Pray in the woods,
Pray when you plough,
Pray in the fields,
Pray when you dig ditches,
Pray in silence
So that no one can see you.

Russian Orthodox

From all that dwells below the skies,
Let faith and hope with joy arise;
Let beauty, truth, and good be sung
Through every land, by every tongue.

Unitarian

O Angel of God
my Guardian dear,
to whom God's love
commits me here,
ever this day
be at my side,
to light, to guard,
to rule and guide.

Christian

O Mother, you are light and your light is everywhere.
Streaming from your body are rays in thousands –
two thousand, a hundred thousand,
tens of millions, a hundred million –
there is no counting their numbers.
It is by you and through you that all things moving
and motionless shine. It is by your light,
O Mother, that all things come to be.

Bhairava Yamala
Hindu

All are nothing but flowers
in a flowering universe.

Nakagawa Soen-roshi
Zen Buddhist

Grandfather,
Look at our brokenness.

We know that in all creation
Only the human family
Has strayed from the Sacred Way.

We know that we are the ones
Who are divided
And we are the ones
Who must come back together
To walk in the Sacred Way.

Grandfather,
Sacred One,
Teach us love, compassion, and honor
That we may heal the earth
And heal each other.

                                        Ojibwa

Blessed art Thou, O Lord our God,
King of the universe,
who has made Thy world lacking in nought,
but hast produced therein
goodly creatures and goodly trees
wherewith to give delight unto the children of men.

Jewish

O our mother the earth, O our father the sky,
Your children are we, and with tired backs
We bring you gifts that you love,
Then weave for us a garment of brightness;
May the warp be the white light of morning,
May the weft be the red light of evening,
May the fringes be the falling rain,
May the border be the standing rainbow.
Thus weave for us a garment of brightness
That we may walk fittingly where the grass is green,
O our mother the earth, O our father the sky!

Tewa Pueblo

O Master of the Earth,
You live without growing old.
You cover everything like the sky.
Give me the joy of understanding You
As the earth and the sky understand You.

Zhuangzi
Taoist

Thank you for the world so sweet,
Thank you for the food we eat,
Thank you for the birds that sing,
Thank you, God, for everything.

Christian

Air is our Master, water our father,
and the great earth our mother.
Day and night are the female and male nurses
in whose lap the whole universe plays.

Guru Nanak
Sikh

Peace is every step.
The shining red sun is my heart.
Each flower smiles with me.
How green, how fresh all that grows.
How cool the wind blows.
Peace is every step.
It turns the endless path to joy.

Thich Nhat Hanh
Zen Buddhist

Earth teach me stillness
   as the grasses are stilled with light.
Earth teach me suffering
   as old stones suffer with memory.
Earth teach me humility
   as blossoms are humble with beginning.
Earth teach me caring
   as the mother who secures her young.
Earth teach me courage
   as the tree which stands all alone.
Earth teach me limitation
   as the ant which crawls on the ground.
Earth teach me freedom
   as the eagle which soars in the sky.
Earth teach me resignation
   as the leaves which die in the fall.
Earth teach me regeneration
   as the seed which rises in the spring.
Earth teach me to forget myself
   as melted snow forgets its life.
Earth teach me to remember kindness
   as dry fields weep with rain.

Ute

The Lord bless you and keep you:
The Lord make his face to shine upon you,
  and be gracious to you:
The Lord lift up his countenance upon you,
  and give you peace.

Numbers 6: 24 - 26

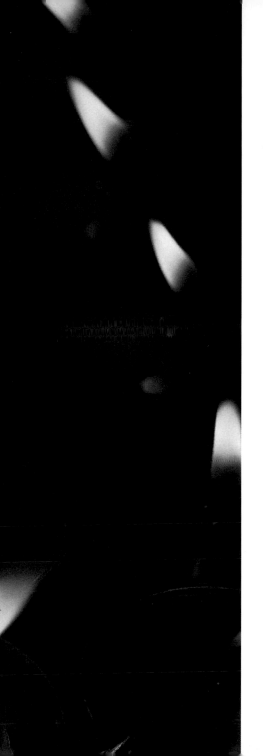

Blessed art Thou, O Lord our God,
King of the universe,
who makest the bands of sleep
to fall upon mine eyes
and slumber upon mine eyelids.

May it be Thy will, O Lord my God,
and God of my fathers,
to suffer me to lie down in peace
and to let me rise up again in peace.

Jewish

Now I lay me down to sleep.
I pray Thee, Lord, my soul to keep.
Your love be with me through the night
And wake me with the morning light.

Christian

Notes on the Prayers

Editor's note: This book reaches across many traditions and cultures, but, inevitably, not all traditions could be included. The photographs and prayers were selected and combined to convey the universality of spiritual experience among the world's peoples. Out of respect for the Islamic faith, Muslim prayers were omitted because the Islamic tradition does not make use of visual images.

The notes below follow the order of the prayers in the book. It is hoped that adults will use these notes to help young readers achieve a greater understanding of the prayers.

Zuni prayer: The opening prayer is taken from the ancient *Night Chant of the Zuni,* which has been intoned for centuries by the indigenous people of the southwestern United States. The night chant celebrates the power of light, both in a physical sense, as the sun whose power ensures the warmth and light necessary for living things to grow, and in a spiritual sense, as the light whose power banishes the darkness of ignorance, giving us a greater awareness of our true nature. The theme of light (symbolized by the sun) as the dispeller of ignorance is common to religious traditions throughout the world.

Russian Orthodox prayer: An ancient Christian faith, the Russian Orthodox religion places great emphasis on the appreciation of beauty in nature, music, and art. This tradition also places the highest value on prayer and its relevance to every aspect of daily life. This prayer connects our everyday activities and the rhythms of the natural world with the rhythms of our inner life.

Unitarian prayer: The Unitarian tradition offers individuals a way to discover wholeness and a sense of underlying unity in life by understanding that truth comes to us from many different sources, especially from our own life experience. This prayer expresses the Unitarian reverence for the earth and the value placed on sharing and on openness to the beliefs of others.

Christian prayer: The idea that each of us has a guardian angel to help us on our journey through life is a traditional belief of the Catholic faith, but it may well have roots that reach back before Christianity, since the idea of spirit guides or guardians is common to many ancient cultures.

The Bhairava Yamala: The numerous gods and goddesses of the Hindu tradition represent the many ways in which we perceive and experience the divine. In India, the divine was originally seen as maternal. Excerpted from an ancient Hindu scripture, *The Bhairava Yamala,* this prayer celebrates the divine mother's awesome power, which radiates throughout the manifest world. The light of the divine mother represents not only physical light as we perceive it, but also the energy that enlightens consciousness and vitalizes all living things.

Nakagawa Soen-roshi: Nakagawa Soen-roshi was one of the first Zen teachers to introduce Buddhism to the West. Zen is a Japanese school of Buddhism that does not separate the sacred from the secular. It focuses on simplicity and on a life which is in harmony with nature. Along with describing a particular moment in summer, this poem celebrates the continual flowering of energy throughout the universe.

Ojibwa prayer: An indigenous people of North America, the Ojibwa live in parts of the northern United States and southern Canada. For the Ojibwa and other Native Americans, sacred teachings are expressed in the laws of nature, and the natural world is considered to be the dwelling place of the Great Spirit. According to Native American belief, contentment and well-being are possible only if we follow the Sacred Way of nature.

Jewish prayer: This celebratory prayer is traditionally recited each year at the first blossoming of trees in spring.

Tewa Pueblo prayer: The Tewa are one of the many Pueblo communities who inhabit the southwestern United States. Family is the cornerstone of Tewa culture, but all humans are also seen as children of the earth as mother and the sky as father. This prayer shows the Tewa's profound respect for the beauty and mystery of the natural world and the importance they place on living in harmony with nature.

Zhuangzi: Zhuangzi lived in the fourth century B.C. and is one of the fathers of Taoism, China's oldest religion. This prayer is recorded in his book of essays, also named *Zhuangzi,* one of the classic texts of Taoism, which regards harmony between humans and the laws of nature as a spiritual ideal.

Christian prayer: Many prayers acknowledge the interdependence of human beings and the forces of nature. This simple Christian grace acknowledges that interdependence by connecting the sweetness of the food we eat with the sweetness of the living world.

Guru Nanak: In the fifteenth century, Guru Nanak founded Sikhism in northern India. Living in troubled times between Hindus and Muslims, he encouraged people to see beyond their religious differences and to have a sense of justice and social responsibility. He taught through poetry and practical example, and his verse forms part of the *Guru Granth Sahib,* a collection of poetry that Sikhs revere and recite from daily.

Thich Nhat Hanh: Thich Nhat Hanh is a Vietnamese Buddhist monk, scholar, poet, and peace activist. Exiled from his country for his peaceful resistance to the Vietnam War, he now lives with the community he founded at Plum Village, Meyrac, France, where he teaches, writes, and gardens. He continues to help Vietnamese refugees and leads retreats in mindful living all over the world. This prayer helps us to understand that peace is not only a social and spiritual ideal; it is also our natural state.

Ute prayer: The Ute are a small, formerly nomadic tribe living in the southwestern United States. For the Ute, as for other Native Americans, the earth must not be controlled or changed, for it is intrinsically beautiful, harmonious, and sacred. If we know how to relate properly to the earth, it will teach us everything we need to know.

Numbers: Numbers is one of the five books of Moses, known collectively as the Pentateuch. It contains a series of instructions given to Moses by God. This blessing is an extremely powerful prayer because, in Judaism, normally it is thought impossible to look upon the face of God and survive.

Jewish prayer: This traditional nighttime prayer asks for peace during the hours of sleep and acknowledges the power of God both as the provider of sleep and restorer of wakefulness. The quality of energy at dawn and dusk make these significant times for prayer in many traditions.

Christian prayer: This prayer is part of Christianity's oral tradition. In simple verse, it expresses the willing surrender of the individual to the divine, giving a special quality to the moments between wakefulness and sleep.

The Sierra Club, founded in 1892 by John Muir, has devoted itself to the study and protection of the earth's scenic and ecological resources — mountains, wetlands, woodlands, wild shores and rivers, deserts and plains. The publishing program of the Sierra Club offers books to the public as a nonprofit educational service in the hope that they may enlarge the public's understanding of the Club's basic concerns. The point of view expressed in each book, however, does not necessarily represent that of the Club. The Sierra Club has some sixty chapters in the United States and Canada. For information about how you may participate in its programs to preserve wilderness and the quality of life, please address inquiries to Sierra Club, 85 Second Street, San Francisco, CA 94105, or visit our website at http://www/sierraclub.org

First U.S. Edition 1997

First published in Great Britain by Barefoot Books Ltd.

Library of Congress Cataloging-in-Publication Data

One earth, one spirit: a child's book of prayers from many faiths and cultures / compiled by Tessa Strickland.
    p. cm.
    Summary: Photographs of children from around the world are combined with more than fifteen prayers from different times and places to celebrate the natural world.
    ISBN 0-87156-978-7
    1. Earth — Religious aspects — Juvenile literature. 2. Children — Prayer-books and devotions. [1.Earth — Religious aspects. 2. Prayers.] 1. Strickland, Tessa.
BL438.2.056 1997
291.4'33—dc21
96-40387

Graphic design by Tom Grzelinski

Printed in Singapore

10 9 8 7 6 5 4 3 2 1

SOURCES AND ACKNOWLEDGMENTS

Many thanks to everyone who helped in the creation of *One Earth, One Spirit,* and in particular to Andrea Andriotto and Caroline English, for painstaking picture research; to Tom Grzelinski, who learned that book design is not always as straightforward as it seems; to Gopinder Panesar and Nancy Traversy of Barefoot Books; and to Helen Sweetland of Sierra Club Books for Children, San Francisco.

The Photographs

Grateful acknowledgment is made to the following photo agencies and photographers for their permission to reproduce material copyrighted or controlled by them:

© **Robert Harding Picture Library:** child in swing, U.S.A. (p. 10); children holding hands, U.S.A. (p. 22).
© **The Image Bank:** child running into the sunset (p. 30).
© **Don Klumpp/The Image Bank:** girl wading into the ocean, Mexico (jacket, p. 1, and p. 26).
© **Sandra Lousada/Collections:** two children hugging, England (p. 2 and p. 32).
© **Edwin Maynard/The Tibet Image Bank:** butterlamps, Tibet (p. 34).
© **F. Nock/Hutchison Picture Library:** Kogi Steps, Colombia (p. 4 and p. 16).
© **Pictor International:** Peruvian father with child (p. 20).
© **G.A. Rossi/The Image Bank:** Balinese girl in temple (p. 12 and p. 38).
© **Irene Slegt/The Tibet Image Bank:** Tibetan monks blowing horns (p. 8).
© **Sobel & Klonsky/The Image Bank:** young farm girl riding horse cart, U.S.A. (p. 6).
© **Topham PicturePoint:** boy with bowl of fish, Zaire (p. 24).
© **Jenny Woodcock/Reflections Photolibrary:** child with cherry blossoms, England (p. 18); child sleeping, England (p. 36).
© **David Woodfall/Woodfall Wild Images:** traditional hay meadow, England (p. 14).
© **Yan Lun Jean Yves/The Image Bank:** Chinese children in rice field (p. 28).

The Prayers

Grateful acknowledgment is made to the following authors and publishers for permission to reprint material copyrighted by them:

William Collins Sons & Co. Ltd., for excerpt from *The Bible: Revised Standard Version.* Copyright © 1973 by Division of Christian Education of the National Council of the Churches of Christ in the United States of America.

Harper San Francisco, for an excerpt from *The Name of My Beloved: Verses of the Sikh Gurus,* translated and introduced by Nikki-Gurinder Kaur Singh (1995).

Parallax Press, Berkeley, California, for an excerpt from *The Long Road Turns to Joy: A Guide to Walking Meditation,* by Thich Nhat Hanh (1996).

University of Chicago Press, for an excerpt from *The Tewa World,* by Alfonso Ortiz. Copyright © 1964 by University of Chicago Press. All rights reserved.

Every effort has been made to contact the holders of copyrighted material. If notified, the Publishers will rectify any omissions in future editions.